Who Wears The Tux?

The Original Great American Dyke Quiz (accept no substitutes!)

Julia Willis

Banned Books
Austin, Texas

A BANNED BOOK

Published in the United States of America
By BANNED BOOKS
An Imprint of Edward-William Publishing Company
Number 292, P.O. Box 33280, Austin, Texas 78764

ISBN 0-934411-30-1

The illustrations in this book come from the following copyrighted books from Dover Publications: *Women: A Pictorial Archive From Nineteenth-Century Sources*, selected by Jim Harter, © 1978; *Handbook of Early Advertising Art*, Clarence P. Hornung, © 1982; *Goods and Merchandise: A Cornucopia of Nineteenth-Century Cuts*, compiled and arranged by William Rowe, © 1982; *Ready-To-Use Old-Fashioned Romantic Cuts*, edited by Carol Belanger Grafton, © 1987; *Picture Sourcebook for Collage and Decoupage*, edited by Edmund V. Gillon, Jr., © 1974; *Ready-To-Use Gibson Girl Illustrations*, selected and arranged by Carol Belanger Grafton, © 1989; *Ready-To-Use Old-Fashioned Animal Cuts*, Carol Belanger Grafton, © 1987; *Ready-To-Use Old-Fashioned Sports Illustrations*, designed by Carol Belanger Grafton, © 1988; *Scenes From the Nineteenth-Century Stage in Advertising Woodcuts*, selected and edited by Stanley Appelbaum, © 1977; *Ready-To-Use Old-Fashioned Transportation Cuts, edited by Carol Belanger Grafton, © 1987; Curious Woodcuts of Fanciful and Real Beasts*, Konrad Gesner, © 1971.

For Laurel,
who almost always has the right answer.

Contents

Introduction

Welcome to WHO WEARS THE TUX?—The Original Great American Dyke Quiz (accept no substitutes!). May I suggest that you sharpen your pencils, put on your thinking caps, please refrain from looking over the shoulder of the lovely woman in front of you, and begin. Try to think of this not as a test but rather a thrilling adventure (and I'll switch my metaphor in midstream solely for the benefit of you woodsy types—I personally am and shall always remain among the ranks of the rustically challenged): yes, come with us now as we make our way along the Old Sapphic Trail, over hill and dale and whatnot, observing the habits and habitats of the lesbian (red-breasted or otherwise) as she is found in nature. Having spent many fruitful years absorbed in my study of this fascinating creature and knowing this primrose path the way I do, there is much this questionnaire will reveal to you (and more you will reveal to others) as we explore these hitherto uncharted nether regions of women's hearts, souls, minds, and dietary restrictions. But let me warn you at the outset: there will be subject matter that may displease you, offend you, or even cause you to laugh, chuckle, roll upon either the floor or a close friend, or in some other manner display great emotion or bold passion. If you have no desire for this sort of brash behavior, this little book is not for you. If, on the other hand, you relish the idea of wisdom tempered by absurdity, or you're just skimming through these pages for the erotically charged stuff—why, rip off your clothes and hop right in! (And if those clothes are not too badly ripped, are of a bright and sunny disposition, and would fit a mature size twelve, please send them right along to me in care of my publisher.)

Our delightful excursion is divided into four parts, each of which may or may not be taken separately (after meals or before bedtime). The answers to the questions can be found at the bottom of the page, upside down (ah-ah-ah, don't peek). Suggestions for scoring and what sort of honors to bestow upon the winners, along with my hearty congratulations, are in the back. Needless to say, any flora, fauna, or tidbits of advice you gather on our road to cosmic dykedom will be entirely your own responsibility.

So—good luck, don't forget to wear sensible shoes—and yes, dears, we will be holding hands around the campfire tonight.

Julia Willis
Boston, Massachusetts
January 1990

PART I

How It All Began: A Brief History Of Dykedom Past And Present, In Which We Take A Look At The Lesbian Of Yesteryear And Yesterday, Digging Up A Few Roots And Dishing A Little Dirt

The Bigger Bang Theory

Where did we come from and how did we get here?

A. We come from the Amazon planet Sis in the Labia Majora galaxy. Our mission is to create a welcome and loving diversion in an otherwise primitive and generally uninhabitable environment known as Earth. Our soul identities are made manifest in a certain percentage of all female babies born to human parents.

B. Well, one time Lilith shoved Adam off her and got up and said "That's enough of this" and left. She was later spotted living with a woman who sold camels down in Babylon.

C. We used to be dolphins until evolution gave us the clitoris. Then all hell broke loose.

D. It was just one of those things.

E. We don't recall.

The answer (and although I have no definitive proof, my sources are entirely reputable) is A. Now doesn't this explain a lot?

Batter Up!

The mystique surrounding women and softball is powerful. Where did the name originate?

A. On the playing fields of Eton.

B. In ancient times, when Amazons ritually tossed the heads of their enemies around a circle to celebrate victory over the patriarchy.

C. Next to the Piedmont Regional High School in Pickens, South Carolina, in 1911, when Miss Minnie Mae Moore and her "chum" Miss Sara Sperling started the first Maiden Ladies' Saturday Softball League, and the girls came from six counties to gaze upon Minnie Mae and her pitcher's mound.

D. None of the above.

The answer is B. Eventually they switched from heads to a more blatantly offensive rounded body part—hence the name "*softball*." Had this change not occurred, many of you would now belong to softhead teams.

Gay Paree

How much do you know about the artsy dykes running rampant in Paris in the twenties (and even earlier)? Which of these statements is *false*?

A. Gertrude and Alice called each other "Kitty" and "Pussy."

B. Colette was once an exotic dancer.

C. Renee Vivien the poet had herself delivered to Natalie Barney in a coffin.

D. Josephine Baker made love to Greta Garbo on the steps of the Eiffel Tower.

E. Djuna Barnes always wore a great black cape and carried a formidable cane with a silver fox's head on top.

Well, it's D that has never been documented as fact. But if you want to believe it, or just picture it in your mind's eye, who am I to stop you?

Why Do Fools Fall In Love?

Pretend it's the fifties again (sometimes you'd almost swear it was, anyway). You've just graduated from Women's College in Greensboro and moved to New York City and found a place to live in Greenwich Village on Jane Street. Now you're all set for romance — but when you walk into a real honest-to-goodness lezzy bar, your arrival is greeted by puzzled frowns. What's wrong?

A. Your slip is showing.

B. No one can tell if you're a butch or a femme.

C. You're carrying a copy of *Finnegan's Wake* under your arm and trying to look intellectual.

D. You were so nervous you drank half a bottle of gin before you left the apartment.

B. Rules were rules and roles were roles back then. Even the alternative lifestyles had their limitations. Now you only wear jockey shorts if you want to.

Stonewall

"Those who do not learn the lessons of history are doomed to repeat them." Someone famous said that. I think it was either Oscar Wilde or Barney Frank. Anyway, there are some events in our history we ought never to forget. What does "Stonewall" mean to you?

A. Some guy in the Civil War who got shot by his own men.

B. A favorite tactic of any Republican administration.

C. The bar on Christopher Street where, on June 27th, 1969, the drag queens stood up to the cops and the modern gay rights movement began.

D. One of those structures Robert Frost said made good neighbors.

C. The other answers are approximately correct, but there will always be only one Stonewall. So God bless Mama and Grandma and Scooter and all the drag queens . . . .

The Law

Which of the following statements most accurately reflects what American law has to say about lesbianism?

A. "Don't knock it if you haven't tried it."

B. "Just don't do it in the street and scare the horses."

C. "Well, we were going to make you all wear these big scarlet L's across your chests so we'd know who was who, but then we realized we might get you mixed up with the bleeding-heart liberals who are already wearing them. So we'll use these all-purpose Q's instead."

D. "Those sodomy laws aren't just for faggots, you know, so all you lesbians and heterosexuals better straighten up and fly right, too. It's strictly the old missionary position, or we march into your bedrooms and haul you off to the hoosegow, pronto."

E. "No minority, including gay men and lesbians, shall be discriminated against. Period."

F. "But what exactly could two women do?"

Because at this point E is the law in so few states, and D is the law in so many, D is the answer. However, to my knowledge there has never been a law against sending a woman flowers and kissing her tenderly on the mouth, so do it well and frequently with no fear of reprisal.

Psychiatry

What has the field of psychiatry concluded concerning lesbianism?

A. Freud: "Overt homosexuality in women is the result of masturbation. A woman who has discovered her own clitoris is a woman who will seek the clitoris in others."

B. Anna Freud: "Dorothy and I are just good friends, and what business is it of yours, anyway?"

C. Jung: "Animus, anima—however you girls work it out is okay with me."

D. The "expert" sexologist your parents sent you to as late as 1970: "So—you dress like a butch, but you act like a femme. Um—so which are you?"

E. American Psychological Association, circa 1980: "All right, all right, we'll grudgingly admit it's just an alternate lifestyle."

F. All of the above statements are reasonably accurate.

F is the answer. However, "reasonably accurate" does not mean true. (Anna Freud spent fifty years with her companion Dorothy Burlingham, but she flatly denied having any sexuality at all. Well, with a daddy like Sigmund, how can we blame her?)

Religion

Which of the following Judeo-Christian statements regarding lesbianism was never made?

A. Leviticus: "Jehovah is definitely not into faggots or dykes or eating pigs or shellfish, and He really can't stand the Queen of Heaven that everybody around here used to worship, but He is rather fond of concubines and chattel. So watch it, okay? Because he's very wrathful."

B. Mary Magdalene, The Apocrypha: "Martha and I are just good friends, and what business is it of yours, anyway?"

C. St. Paul, First Corinthians: "Ooh—just thinking about it turns me on, so it must be incredibly sinful."

D. The Torah: "Not only do I thank God every morning that I wasn't born a woman, I thank Him every night I wasn't born a lesbian. Hey—why are Sarah and Rachel over there holding hands and smiling?"

E. Pope John Paul II: "The more you suffer, the better God likes it. Hey—why are those nuns over there holding hands and smiling?"

F. The 700 Club: "All you queers are sinning, and we love sinners. So please call the number on your screen and pledge to help this ministry. Hey—why are those phone operators over there holding hands and smiling?"

G. The Episcopals: "Maybe we ought to let them get married. Then no one could say we weren't being nice."

All of the above statements have been made (yea, verily), except B. Mary Magdalene never said she and Martha were *just* good friends.

Politics

Word connotations often change with the generations (as in the case of "yup," originally a word Gary Cooper used as the opposite of "nope") or even the seasons. At this very moment, what does "politics" mean to you?

A. Who you voted for.

B. What you're protesting.

C. Who you associate with and whether or not they eat dead animals on a bun with lettuce and mayo.

D. Who you're sleeping with.

The correct answer here depends on your age. If you are between the ages of thirty and fifty, you should have answered B, C, or D. If you are under thirty or over fifty, you are much more likely, unfortunately, to have answered A. If in either case you gave an answer not corresponding to your age group's expected response, I guess that's all right, too. What the hell—politics and correctness are both so subjective.

Lesbian Novels

It's very important that you maintain a historical perspective on lesbian writing *before* the recent rash of fiction in every genre from mystery to romance to roman à clef to social commentary. Why? Because, dear readers (she said, adjusting her pince-nez), you will learn how far we have come in creating a variety of more positive role models, and you will see how far we have yet to go on the road to great and lasting literature. It will be *good* for you — and I expect to see your papers on my desk by Friday. Meanwhile, from the following plot descriptions, pick the one which corresponds to the narrative action in the 1928 novel *The Well of Loneliness.*

A. Two women run away together and make a homestead for themselves in rural New York State, back when the far West was Buffalo.

B. Laura spends several miserable years with a butch named Beebo who pretends she was raped to keep Laura interested, and then somehow Laura ends up married (to a nice mixed-up faggot) and expecting a baby.

C. A picaresque novel of the adventures of a young Horatia Alger-type: everything she touches turns to gold and every woman she touches turns to putty in her hands. Based on the real-life megalomania of the author.

D. A girl named Stephen falls in love with another British ambulance driver in WWI but eventually sacrifices her own happiness to see that her one true love is safely married to a nice boy.

E. Jan and her friends drink tea and sip brandy and wander around thinking how wrong it all is and how very, very lovely. Sigh.

All right, pens down. You should have written D in the space provided (what space?). How many of you got it? Tsk, tsk. D is *The Well of Loneliness* by Radclyffe Hall, whose friends called her John (OK . . . .). She and Lady Trowbridge lived in the English countryside and raised dachshunds. A quick run-down on the others (and you may have an extra point for knowing two or more): A is *Patience and Sarah*, an early seventies novel by Isobel Miller, B *Women in the Shadows* (1959) by Ann Bannon, C the classic *Rubyfruit Jungle* (also early seventies) by Rita Mae Brown, and E is *We Too Are Drifting* (1935) by Gail Wilhelm.

Lesbians On Film

Movie censorship forbade any references to "taboo" subjects including lesbianism from the early thirties into the sixties, when restrictions were lifted and lesbians came onto the screen — still nearly unrecognizable as human beings. Who will be most remembered for her truly awful portrayal of a lesbian in a mainstream motion picture?

A. Barbara Stanwyck, playing a crusty madam in a New Orleans brothel with a bad case of the hots for one of her girls (played by Capucine, an actress who always seemed dubbed, even when she wasn't), in "Walk on the Wild Side."

B. Sandy Dennis, as the femme who whines so loudly and so long that it's honestly a relief when the tree falls on her, in "The Fox."

C. Anne Heywood, probably the most inept butch in the history of cinema (it's almost a shame that tree doesn't get her, too), also in "The Fox."

D. Either of the two French twits starring in "Therese and Isabelle," a salute to girls everywhere who ran screaming from boarding school into a respectable married state.

E. Raquel Welch, in an unforgettable screen appearance as the Greek poet Sappho, in "Women of Lesbos."

F. Shirley MacLaine, giving her all as poor Martha who practically in the same breath declares her love for Karen (Audrey Hepburn) and hangs herself (not what you'd call a very positive role model), in "The Children's Hour."

G. Mercedes McCambridge, doubly nominated for her roles as the leather-clad sadist in "Touch of Evil" and the gingham-clad homophobe in love with Joan Crawford (which is, of course, why she is *so* determined to kill her) in an odd (and I do mean odd) Western, "Johnny Guitar."

H. Susannah York, as the helpless homebody who eats cigars and drinks bathwater in "The Killing of Sister George."

I. Two women who should have known better.

The answer is I, and the two women Alexis Smith and Melina Mercouri, for their horrifying portrayal of a pair of drooling, lascivious, and highly unattractive lesbians (and by this I do not mean they looked ugly, but that they gave off such an unsavory, unwholesome attitude toward each other it was enough to make your skin crawl—honest) in the 1975 bomb "Once Is Not Enough." But it was—it was more than enough. Oh, and concerning answer E, Raquel never made a movie called "Women of Lesbos." But we can dream, can't we?

The Girls

How do you relate to the word "girl" or "girls"?

A. As the sexist equivalent of "boy" to blacks.

B. As who your mother invited over to play bridge and eat brownies.

C. As what Lucy called Ethel.

D. As all of the above.

E. As all of the above, and much, much more.

The answer is E. It is our duty, as "wimmin," to reclaim those sincere and loving properties inherent in "girls" as it was used by Lucy and our mothers, much as we have reclaimed and re-defined other terms once considered to be derogatory (such as "dyke," "lipgloss," and "cheeseburger").

Straight Girls

You have come out to a straight friend at work. Does she:

A. treat you exactly the way she did before?

B. act uncomfortable around you?

C. tell other co-workers, who then make life miserable for you until you quit the job?

D. begin to flirt with you and ask you out for a drink and confess to you that she has slept with a hundred and fifty-seven men and never had an orgasm in her entire life?

The answer is D. Although the other answers are remote possibilities, you can almost set your watch by the needy straight women who will show up on your doorstep looking for orgasms. Get a deadbolt lock.

Straight Boys

You become friends with a straight boy, a nice fellow, a — dare we say it? — liberal. At some point, after you have come out to him, he says, "Well, I'm just curious. Have you ever slept with a man, or gone out with one, or anything? I'm just curious." What do you reply?

A. "Oh, yes—I was even married once, to a guy very much like you."

B. "Yeah, I lived with a man before I came out. We still exchange cards at Christmas."

C. "Well, I slept with a few guys in college, but I never got serious. It was just a physical thing."

D. "I dated a little in high school, but boys just never turned me on."

E. "No, never, ever. Nothing personal, but just the thought of being touched by a man is so absolutely repugnant to me I become physically ill. Please don't bring it up again, okay?"

Say E. I don't care whether any one of answers A–D applies to your situation. Even if one of them fits you like a glove, don't—I repeat, do *not* tell him so. Lie, lie, lie. Anything other than answer E will give him hope, and a straight boy who has hope in his heart and a lesbian at his side is a worrisome sight to behold.

Faggots

There is so much we have in common with our gay brethren, and yet there will be always be differences in the way we live and the things we appreciate passionately. Which of the following concepts best captures our inability to perceive life through the eyes of faggots, and vice versa?

A. Their greater likelihood of economic freedom.

B. Their higher visibility in politics, the media, etc.

C. Our general tendency toward monogamy.

D. Our PMS.

E. Judy Garland.

D. Until a faggot has walked a mile with my cramps, we will never truly understand one another.

Women's Bars, or "It'll Look A Lot Better Once We Get That Ceiling Fixed"

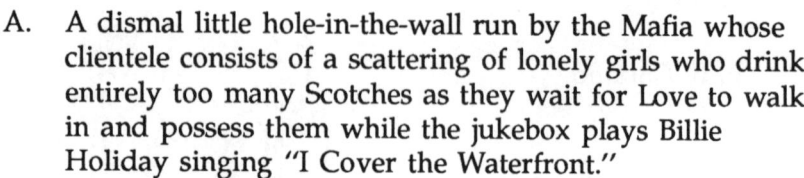

What's a "women's bar" really like?

A. A dismal little hole-in-the-wall run by the Mafia whose clientele consists of a scattering of lonely girls who drink entirely too many Scotches as they wait for Love to walk in and possess them while the jukebox plays Billie Holiday singing "I Cover the Waterfront."

B. A converted firehouse with concrete floors and folding chairs which doubles as a food co-op during the week, and on Saturday nights they push the wilted produce and the sacks of brown rice into the corner, hire a female duo called Rosemary and Thyme that plays Laura Nyro covers, and serve apple juice and carob brownies to women who have made a conscious decision to devote one hundred percent of their energies, "including their sexual energies," to other women.

C. An uptown establishment complete with revolving disco ball, dance floor made of panels of colored lights, strobe effects, and ear-splitting speakers arranged to maximize insight into the length and breadth of Donna Summer's orgiastic moans. The bouncers wear leather, a membership card is de rigueur, and the stalls in the bathroom are used for arcane rituals involving rolled-up dollar bills, pocket mirrors, and mysterious sniffing sounds.

D. A drug-free, smoke-free environment with a restaurant upstairs which specializes in homemade pasta, delicate cream sauces, California zinfandel, and a chocolate mousse pie (with chocolate chips and chocolate graham cracker crust and a chocolate truffle garnish with chocolate whipped cream topping), and a room downstairs that alternates cabaret acts with dance nights featuring a rap DJ named Tina T. on Wednesdays and Sundays.

E. Any combination of the above.

The answer is E. A–D represent the quintessential women's spaces of the previous four decades, but I'm sure variations on them all still exist and will continue so long as there's a market for nostalgia, style, political correctness, and closets.

California, Here I Come

Why do many gay women live in San Francisco?

A. It smells better than New York City.

B. Its Old World ambience makes L.A. look like a truck stop on I-40.

C. Because so many gay women live there.

D. They enjoy being able to turn to a lover and say, "Darling, what can I tell you—the earth moved."

E. They can't leave, because they've forgotten where they came from.

In this quiz's opinion, the answer is E. There's something in the fog that inhibits that part of the brain which would remember places like Indiana. This is not necessarily a bad thing.

New York, New Yuck

Why do many gay women live in New York City?

A. They're hoping one day to catch a glimpse of Ivana Trump.

B. They like to step in dogshit and over the homeless.

C. Because so many gay women live there.

D. They relish the idea of being mugged.

E. They all own galleries in Soho.

F. They're all going to be rich and famous.

C. Of course, if they wanted to they could all decide to go and live somewhere else. Somewhere civilized, like Seattle. But they won't. A tough, perverse lot, these girls.

Are You "That Way?"

Many of you may think this is an unnecessary question. After all, if you aren't "out" as a lesbian, what are you doing with this book? Well, there could be many reasons. Which of the following sounds like a woman fighting her own nature?

A. "Oh, I'm not gay or anything. My sister is. She gave me this book to look at after I told her I had this wicked crush on Tracy Chapman."

B. "I'm doing a paper for my sociology class."

C. "I need information to prove how insidious this so-called alternate lifestyle can be when I call up the talk radio stations and condemn homosexuals to the darkest pit in hell."

D. "I just found it on the subway. Honey, I can't even read—I'm only looking at the pictures."

They're all suspect answers, so give yourself half-credit for A, B, or D, but the best answer is C. This woman (and so many like her) is suffering from what we doctors call the "Oh, I Couldn't Be" Syndrome. It is rarely fatal, but often highly obnoxious.

PART II

Falling In Love,
or
"How To Go About Finding Someone To Share Your Bed, Your Life, And Someday Maybe Even Your Gas Bill"

Experience: Not The Best Teacher

When you hear someone say she hasn't had much experience with women, often her tone will be rather apologetic, as if with experience she'll somehow get better. How does the experience of having many lovers in her past change a woman's present perspective?

A. It makes her fantastic in bed.

B. It makes her pretty cynical.

C. It makes her very jumpy.

D. It makes her very happy.

E. It makes her nose grow.

Women who think they're fantastic in bed will answer A, because that's their rationale for having so many lovers—to keep in practice. However, the answer is B. In many cases a woman's cynicism has been known to increase in direct proportion to the number of times someone has whispered in her ear, "I want to be with you like this forever."

Meeting In A Bar

A partying group of girls comes in together and sits at a big table in the corner. You're dying to meet one of them. How do you approach her? You:

A. stand at the bar and give her what is known as "the long look."

B. try to find out who she is by asking around and call her the next day.

C. walk over to the table, say "Would anyone like to dance?" and hope she accepts the invitation first.

D. walk over to the table, motion to her, and point to a quiet spot where you can introduce yourselves.

E. walk over to the table and yell "Mind if I sit down?"

F. do nothing, then go home and kick yourself to sleep.

D if you're really brave, B if you're not. The problem is that whole table full of girls. There's something about traveling in packs that regresses even the best of us back to the level of a junior high school clique.

Meeting At The Gym

It's been said that the fitness centers of today are the queer bars of yesteryear. And not only is the lighting better but in order to wake up hung over the next morning you'd have to eat at least half a tube of Ben-Gay. So, is the health club or gym or YWCA a good place to meet the woman of your dreams? Perhaps, but only if:

A. your gym teacher used to let you wear her whistle.

B. you don't tend to turn beet red in the face and sweat profusely.

C. you feel you can tell a lot about someone by the way she watches herself in the mirror.

D. you are stimulated by the smell of chlorine and old socks.

The answer is A. The key words here are "woman of your dreams," and studies indicate that those of you who as adolescents lay in bed at night fantasizing about Miss Kruger (especially after you saw her riding home from school one day with her roommate Miss Allen) will pick the correct response 99% of the time. The remaining 1% of you are still too busy fantasizing to answer some silly question.

Meeting At A Party

You go to a party with friends. After having a long, boring conversation about vitamins with an amateur nutritionist in the kitchen, you walk back down the hall and suddenly, across a crowded room, there she is — that woman of your dreams. How often does this sort of thing really happen?

A. Constantly.

B. More often than you might think.

C. Only very occasionally.

D. Almost never.

A. It happens constantly, all the time. But when it does happen (constantly), she's always looking the other way, suffering from major heartbreak, leaving with someone else, or moving to Mozambique on Monday.

Meeting Through The Personals

You decide to seek romance through a personal ad. Which description of yourself will elicit the most favorable response?

A. "Straight-appearing, well-hung, hot and horny."

B. "Divorced woman, hoping to explore a different avenue."

C. "Lonely, shy, love dogs, live in Woonsocket, Rhode Island."

D. "Attractive LF, casually seeking someone with shared interest in good books, good movies, and good times for friendship and/or possible relationship."

This is a trick question. A will attract a big gay male following, B will get you in a lot of trouble (drawing in those women who love a challenge), C will leave you lonely in Woonsocket*, and D is what everybody else who's not a boy, straight, or in Woonsocket would say. If you chose any of these answers, you lose a turn and win a free trial subscription to "The Wishing Well."

*and you know, there are either a lot of lonely dykes in Woonsocket, or one very persistent one—I would swear I've seen that same ad for years now, and I wish she or all of them would pack up the dogs and move to a friendlier town. Please ....

No Stereotypes Need Apply

When you close your eyes and picture her (the woman of your dreams), is it important that she be:

A. any special size or shape?

B. of any particular ethnic, racial, religious, or educational background?

C. a good cook?

D. equipped with any physical or sensory challenges?

E. not more than several years younger or older than you?

C. Yes, it is important that she be a good cook. I mean, not that there's anything *wrong* with someone who can't cook, but you know—it might be hard to get used to. I mean, you know how those bad cooks always are. But don't get me wrong, I'm not prejudiced or anything . . . .

Lawyers Court, But Therapists Charge

The profession of a potential loved one is probably not something you give a lot of thought to, except perhaps to say "I wouldn't want someone in *my* field" or "It would *have* to be someone in my field." But what a woman does for a living can be just a job or a very big part of her life. Which of the following professions would most significantly affect the course of a relationship, for better or worse?

A. Doctor.

B. Computer programmer.

C. Telephone linesperson.

D. Teacher.

E. Chemist.

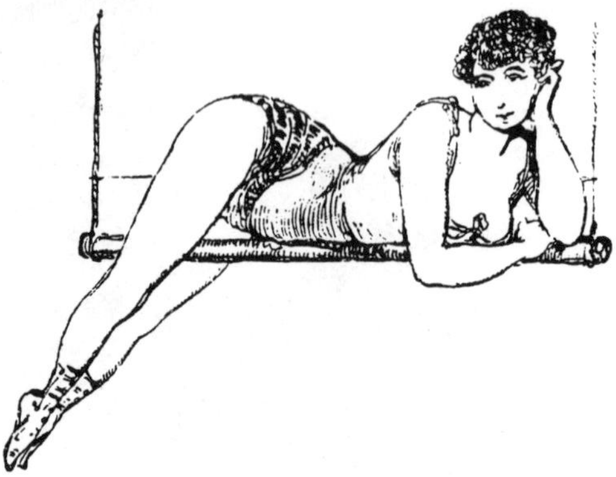

The answer is C. Not that she will bring her work home with her, but I don't think it would be an exaggeration to say that a woman who climbs telephone poles all day will have remarkably strong thighs (the better to hold you with, my dear!).

Age Gaps: "Elvis Who?"

You're forty-one and she's only twenty-six. What is the crucial difference between you?

A. Her skin has more elasticity.

B. You were at Woodstock.

C. She will turn to you one day while reading a gay history book and ask in amazement if it's really illegal to be gay.

D. You are gradually beginning to appreciate the concept of a pension plan.

E. Her parents are still playing tennis and yours are forgetting where they left their teeth.

The answer is B. It doesn't matter how you try to explain it—she will never truly understand the sixties. And that's heavy. It's even far-out.

Ms. Manners On Facial Hair

At yet another dance you meet a woman who is obviously cultivating a beard or moustache. Do you:

A. ask her to dance?

B. ask her how long the pre-op stage will last?

C. ask her what brand of fertilizer she's using?

D. ask her if she and Wayne Newton have the same birth-mother?

The answer is A. You may ask her to dance. It's up to her to bring up the subject of pre-op or fertilizer or genetic background. However, if you enjoy the dance, it would then be acceptable to inquire whether she sleeps with her whiskers over or under the covers.

Common Interests

All dating services (and most of you who are actively looking on your own) attempt to match women who have those ever-popular "similar interests." This is not necessarily a guarantee that two individuals will be compatible. A "similar interest" in which of the following would most likely lead to disaster?

A. Sex.

B. Drugs.

C. Rock 'n roll.

D. Fast cars.

E. Fast women.

F. Frozen yogurt.

You may have half-credit for B or E, but F is the correct response. Once you start arguing over who got the biggest helping or who finished the pint in the freezer and whether or not there was only a tablespoon left, you're already on the road to ruin.

Odd Hygiene Facts #1

You've led a fairly conservative life, first in school and then working in a bank. Your last lover wore blouses with power bows. When you relocate to a strange Eastern city, you begin to meet women with a wider range of styles, and at a dance during Gay Pride Week one of your new friends introduces you to Gwen. She is attractive, intelligent, artistic — you would love to get to know her better, but one thing really bothers you. She apparently does not use deodorant or make any effort to disguise her personal odors. You've always enjoyed women's smells in moderation, but being within ten feet of Gwen makes your eyes water and your nose-hairs curl. What do you do?

A. Get upwind of her before you pass out.

B. Ask her to go for a walk, hoping she'll air out or put on a jacket.

C. Make a date with her for breakfast to find out how she smells first thing in the morning.

D. Find out where she lives and leave a can of Secret in her mailbox.

E. Tell her frankly that her scent is overpowering.

C. This will at least give you a better idea of when and if she bathes at all. If at nine a.m. you can't manage to eat your omelet across the booth from her, this will definitely be an obstacle to your future happiness with Gwen.

First Words, Lasting Impressions

You may think that when you first meet someone, those crucial first words you say can make all the difference between a love that transcends speech and an affair doomed to sentence fragments. This is why you've stopped going out at night. But blurting out the wrong thing in the beginning doesn't always result in ultimate failure. Only some opening lines are unforgivable. Which of these is?

A. "Are you gay?"

B. "Did you see 'Desert Hearts'?"

C. "I'm sorry. Bootsie only does that to people she really likes."

D. "I've been meaning to get those brakes fixed. Uh—I've called you an ambulance."

E. "I have to say right up front that I'm a confirmed bulimic and proud of it."

The answer is B. I don't know about you, but if I hear one more word about that movie I'm going to track down the negative and cut it up into guitar picks with my bare hands. Or maybe I'll use scissors. (Okay, so it was practically a mainstream picture, it had likeable, sympathetic characters, and nobody died at the end. Of course, it's my opinion that once Kay got to New York and took a good look at the lovely lesbians in the art scene she dropped poor Vivian flat. Once a flirt, always a flirt. But we need more, and I don't mean just another "Horny in the Hay," or "Cream in Your Coffee" video . . . although I'll admit some sleaze does have its moments . . .)

AIDS

You want to discuss safe sex with someone you've just met. What do you say?

A. "I never saw a dental dam, I never hope to see one—
But I can tell you anyhow, I'd rather see than be one."

B. "Are you wearing that enchanting new fragrance, 'Latex Evenings' by Faberge?"

C. "Gee, it's hot in here—guess I'll take my rubber gloves off."

D. "Is that a tube of lubricant in your pocket, or are you just glad to see me?"

E. Any of the above.

The answer is A. A little poetry will add a romantic touch to an otherwise dull consideration of genital hygiene.

Reach Out And Grab Someone

Are talk lines a viable alternative to dating?

A. Only if you're accustomed to paying for sex.

B. Only if you have call-waiting.

C. Only if you prefer fantasy to reality.

D. Only if you don't dial the wrong number and spend an hour trying to become emotionally involved with your sister-in-law.

E. Only if your voice has never been compared to either Butterfly McQueen's or Sylvester Stallone's.

B. Because who knows? While you're frittering away your additional minutes (at 10 cents per) with someone who *says* she has a condo in Aspen, there could be a real woman with a simple studio apartment in Austin desperately trying to contact you. And darling, you might just love her wide open spaces.

Saturday Night Specials

Dating among lesbians has little in common with those peculiar courtship rituals practiced by overt heterosexuals, but what custom have we retained?

A. Dinner and a movie, Dutch treat.

B. Parking the car and saying "Okay, put out or walk home."

C. French kissing that makes your partner gag.

D. Pretending to have a headache.

E. Swearing you have no diseases and promising you'll respect her in the morning.

F. A deep, underlying hatred for your date's gender.

A. (And doesn't that phrase "Dutch treat" always remind you of the story of the little Dutch girl who put her finger in the dyke and saved her whole village? That's funny, it always does me.)

Sex — The First Time With The New Love

This is no one-night stand. You see the real possibility of an ongoing relationship here. You've even gone out a few times without spending the night and really gotten to know her better. Now the moment has arrived. What is the best thing you can do to make sure your initial lovemaking goes smoothly?

A. Take the phone off the hook.

B. Put the cat in the other room.

C. Refrain from laughing when she takes her clothes off and reveals her tattoo.

D. Eat and drink lightly beforehand.

E. Pray that the slats in the bed hold out this time.

These are all good suggestions, but the best is B. The last thing a new lover wants to feel when she's in the throes of passion is a set of playful feline claws sinking into her big toe.

Impressing The Loved One

How do you know when you're trying too hard to impress your new girlfriend?

A. You've given her a present that puts your charge card over its limit.

B. You're taking her to restaurants that have valet parking, when you drive a 1968 Volkswagen.

C. You pretend you're firmly committed to environmental issues, though you really only sent $5 to Greenpeace once.

D. You've found yourself telling her you slept with several famous dykes, when in reality you only asked for their autographs.

E. You've redone your apartment in all grays and whites and spent a fortune on jazz CDs.

F. You jump up in the middle of lovemaking to freshen her Perrier and sprinkle more rose petals on the sheets.

All of these are dead giveaways. You can have a point for any of them. Just don't try and impress her with your score so far.

Impressing Others With The Loved One

When you're introducing your new love to your old friends, what do you secretly hope will impress them?

A. Her fantastic looks.

B. Her absolutely cool attitude.

C. Her fabulously funky wardrobe.

D. Her clever mind and sharp wit.

E. Her bad reputation.

F. Her new car.

I imagine the room will be evenly divided on this one between looks (A) and brains (D). But if the truth be known, wouldn't you all be thrilled to be a nice girl showing off your dangerous woman? The most impressive answer is E.

"This Is It!"

How will you know that your love is "The Love of the Century?"

A. You'll look at her, she'll look at you, and you'll both feel weak down around your knees (or possibly in a spot somewhat higher).

B. Bells will ring.

C. You'll discover you both have a fondness for mint mocha chip *and* wear the same shoe size.

D. She's the only gay single woman left in town.

E. It's been a hundred years, and you're still in love.

C. These days it doesn't take much for us to assume it's the real thing. They just don't make centuries like they used to, I guess.

So — Where's The Ring?

This is something that's almost certain to come up. When are you or the woman you're dating most likely to ask for a commitment (or at least broach the subject)?

A. On the first date.

B. In the middle of your first session of lovemaking.

C. The morning after your first session of lovemaking.

D. Within the first six months.

E. Within the first five years.

F. Within the first millennium.

The answer is D (with half-credit for the more tentative E). Those who bring up commitment much too soon (A) or a little too late (F) are not your average dyke, and those who strongly associate commitment with "going all the way" (B or C) are almost exclusively straight girls.

Unrequited Love

It's been said that there's nothing quite as unrequited as unrequited love. (Now wouldn't that make a good country song?) And so often the fact that a love remains unrequited is simply a matter of bad timing or poor communication. When you recall the One That Got Away (or possibly the Two or Three or Six Dozen), do you think she did because:

A. you never told her how much you loved her?

B. you told her exactly how much you loved her, and it was far too much?

C. she was with someone else when the two of you met?

D. you were with someone else when the two of you met?

E. you were both getting over someone else when the two of you met?

F. she took your bait, swallowed your hook, broke your line, stole your paddle, capsized your dinghy, drowned you in the sea of love, and swam merrily on her way?

Any of these answers could have been the real reason the two of you couldn't make a go of it except F, which is the correct answer. If it's a genuinely unrequited love, you will have romanticized and dramatized the whole thing all out of proportion, and in your mind she will always be the one who escaped scot-free while you were left beached on the shore like a dead baby whale (or an unbiodegradable plastic tampon tube).

Unrequited Love In Others #1

You've just begun dating a very nice woman — bright, attractive, happy with her job, her friends, her apartment, her thighs — in short, a woman who seems to have everything going for her — and yet, there's an edge of sadness in her aura. Soon, she tells you. Five years ago, a woman she was lovers with for only three months left her for another, broke her heart, and moved to California. They have had no contact at all since then. She's tried to go on with her life, she *knows* she has everything going for her, but she hasn't been able to find love with anyone else, and even now the very mention of the word "California" sends a dagger through her heart. Sitting across the table with your hands folded on your arms, lowering your chin and nodding sympathetically as she reveals her painful history, you wonder what you'll do when she stops talking. You decide to:

A. sputter something about a forgotten appointment, raise your arm and yell "Check, please!"

B. moan softly "Oh, God, how do they find me?" as you pour yourself another glass of wine.

C. continue nodding sympathetically as you pour *her* another glass of wine.

D. say "I have an old lover in California, too" and proceed to tell her your sad story, sobbing openly into your cloth napkin.

E. promise her that after a few days in bed with you she won't even remember her own name, let alone the name of that bimbo or that place out West you won't speak of.

The answer is C. You don't want to bolt (A) or insult the girl (B), neither do you want to respond inappropriately by attempting to top her misery with your own (D) or presenting your sexual prowess as the solution to all her problems (E). Just let her have her say. Later, when you're lying in bed alone or with her sweet, sleeping form beside you, you can have yours. And it will probably go something like—"Uh-oh, what am I getting myself into now?"

Unrequited Love In Others #2

When an old acquaintance you haven't seen since college comes up to you at a reunion and, in the presence of her third husband, Bob, says in a loud and enthusiastic voice, "Oh, God, I had the biggest crush on you back then! You were *the* most androgynous person I'd ever met! I used to dream about you every night and when I woke up the sheets were *wringing* wet!" — how do you respond?

A. "That's nice. Have you tried the havarti with dill?"

B. "Oh? I never realized that. I guess we all do silly things when we're so young and innocent."

C. "Ooh—how disgusting! I never wanted to believe all those rumors they were spreading about you, but I guess they were right."

D. "You're kidding! Why, I was thinking the very same thing about you! What a small world—huh, Bob?"

E. "Bob, could you excuse us for a minute? I believe the next dance—is mine."

Almost any answer *except* E will do here. Your response (A through D) would be a matter of individual style. Just stay away from E—don't dance with the woman, or get her phone number to call her later, or do anything to renew the acquaintance. She's obviously playing the same games with Bob (and you, if you let her) that she played with her first two husbands. Steer clear—or, if you prefer beating this type at her own game, ask Bob to dance. Later wave to them both as you drive away.

Smart Dykes, Dumb Choices

You begin to wonder if you just have a talent for falling in love with the wrong woman. Does that mean you tend to fall in love with:

A. women who treat you badly, so you feel rotten and have to go into therapy?

B. women who are already involved with someone else, so you feel rotten and have to go into therapy?

C. women who are straight, so you feel rotten and have to go into therapy?

D. straight women already involved with someone else who treat you badly, so you feel rotten and have to go into therapy?

E. your therapist?

The answer is E. Not that any of the other types are good for you, but to fall in love with your therapist—that requires real talent. And a fine self-destructive urge.

PART III

Staying In Love,
or
"What To Do After Falling In Love,"
or
"The Gas Bill Must Be Paid"

Who Wears The Tux?

The two of you have decided to have a ceremony to declare your love and celebrate your happiness with friends. Assuming neither of you is into role-playing, what should you wear for the festivities?

A. You should both wear tuxedos.

B. You should both wear bridal gowns.

C. You should flip a coin to see who gets to wear which.

D. You should both wear matching white flowing robes and Birkenstock sandals.

E. You should both be naked.

The answer is E. Aren't all those conventional marriage outfits boring and derivative? Of course they are. And as for robes, what is this—a ceremony to declare your love or your vows of chastity? Now, be honest: don't you cherish one another's bodies right along with your minds and hearts and spirits? Of course you do. So, it's simple. You might even suggest nudity as an option for your bridesmaids and guests. And that's what we call true lesbian visibility.

Loads Of Sex

You've been together for almost a month. You're making love every day — sometimes twice a day. How will this affect your relationship later on?

A. Sooner or later you'll miss a day, and it'll be all downhill from then on.

B. By the time you've been together for two months, you'll be making love four times a day—sometimes eight.

C. Eventually you'll be so good together you'll have orgasms just thinking about each other.

D. It will have no discernible effect, other than those big silly grins plastered across your faces.

The answer is B. Lovemaking increases exponentially, so that if you stay together for ten years you'll be making love approximately fifteen thousand times a day, or ten times a minute. This is why so many relationships simply cannot be sustained.

"I'm Getting In At Three A.M. — Can You Pick Me Up?"

We've all known of relationships between women on opposite ends of the state or the country or the planet. We might have been involved in a long-distance romance ourselves. We may even be in one at this very moment. How do you think commuting affects the passion in a relationship?

A. Increases it.

B. Decreases it.

C. Doesn't affect it one way or the other.

D. Depends on how hot you get when the phone bill arrives.

E. Depends on how hot you get in the midst of clear air turbulence at 30,000 feet.

At this point we'll have to say C because it is not clear from the available data whether passion is affected in the long run one way or the other. This is due primarily to the fact that in 65% of long-distance relationships one woman will convince the other to move to her city or town within the first six months, and another 20% will have a big fight over the phone and break up (and when the bill comes will tell AT&T they've never even heard of Tuscaloosa, Alabama). Some of you girls don't realize what we statisticians go through trying to figure you out—and you're not making it any easier.

Living With Roommates

You think you're ready to live together, but one of you wants the other to move in with her and her roommates. What's the most important thing to consider in this situation?

A. Whether her roommates keep hemorrhoidal suppositories in the refrigerator where you'll see them every morning before breakfast.

B. Whether her roommates sing along (off-key) with their favorite performers, up to, and including, Patsy Cline.

C. Whether her roommates, when they have their lovers over, scream "Oh God, oh God, oh God!" so loudly in bed that people stop their cars out on the street because they think they've run over somebody.

D. None of the above.

The answer is D. It really doesn't matter what her roommates do—it's a terrible idea to move in with them. Visiting's fine, but if you live there you'll upset the house balance and they'll miss the way she used to be before you came and monopolized all her spare time and energy, and they'll take it out on you at house meetings. Get your own place. Just the two of you. Or both move in with new roommates. You must trust me on this.

Millie Meets Mr. Muffins, or "How Much Is That Band-Aid In The Window?"

One important aspect of living together involves your pets. Too often they have never met before you move in together — or perhaps you brought your dog Millie over once to spend the night and had to take her home after ten minutes. (She still has a scar across her nose where Mr. Muffins, a normally docile house cat, drew blood.) But you move into the new place anyway, leaving the animals till last. Then you put them inside, shut the door, go out for a bite to eat, and hope for the best. What is going to happen?

A. You'll come home to find the two of them curled up on the sofa together.

B. You'll come home to find them glaring at each other.

C. You'll come home to find Mr. Muffins yowling on top of the refrigerator and Millie cowering behind the sofa.

D. You'll come home to find your new place looks like a tornado hit it and both your pets are lifeless balls of chewed and bloodied fur.

E. You'll decide not to go home.

B, though E would probably be the wisest move. They will glare for days. Eventually they will either curl up on the sofa together or be civil to one another or growl and hiss and continue to make life miserable for everyone. Should the worst happen, buy them tiny little boxing gloves and sell tickets.

Household Chores

You'll wash, she'll dry. You'll take out the garbage, she'll dust, you'll take turns vacuuming. But even a carefully planned program of household duties and responsibilities agreed upon before you move in together will not prepare you for some strange and tedious tasks that must be done on a fairly regular basis. Which of these crucial chores will neither of you have the slightest inclination toward doing until the situation reaches critical mass?

A. Picking the hair out of the bathtub drain.

B. Picking the food out of the kitchen drain.

C. Replacing the batteries in the vibrator.

D. Changing the vacuum cleaner bag.

E. Turning the mattress.

F. Rewinding the message tape on the phone machine.

The answer, surprisingly enough, is C. The other chores all seem a good deal more unpleasant, I know, but I think the problem here is that no one remembers to write "batteries" down on the shopping list. And although neglect in these other areas can lead to clogged drains, dirty rugs, lower back pain, and missed messages, none of these can compare to a long and lonely night with a dying vibrator when your sweetheart's on the road. Or even when she's not.

Money

You belong to the school of thought that says what's mine is yours, and you're all for pooling finances. She wants her own separate savings account, checking account, and change for the tollbooth. Which sort of arrangement would you both be comfortable with?

A. One in which you pay the bills and she reimburses you.

B. One in which she pays the bills and you reimburse her.

C. One in which you take turns paying bills.

D. One in which no one pays the bills.

The answer is D. This is obviously the only way to make you both happy. And when you see how much more money you have at the end of the month, you'll be truly ecstatic.

Cooking And Eating

If your dietary habits don't match, how can you avoid clashing in the kitchen?

A. You can't.

B. Keep two bread boxes—one for whole wheat and one for Wonder.

C. Keep two pantry shelves—one for tahini paste and one for Jif.

D. Keep two refrigerators—one for fresh vegetables and one for frozen sausage pizzas.

E. Keep a futon mattress in the corner opposite the microwave.

E. Pretty soon you'll forget your mouth is also used for eating dinner.

Love Of Chocolate

Yours is a relationship in which both of you absolutely *ADORE* chocolate. Does this love supersede your love of:

A. Goddess?

B. country?

C. Mom's apple pie?

D. each other?

The answer is C. Unless Mom picks them herself, apples these days are too likely to be toxic, mushy, or sadly overpriced. However, if Mom made a chocolate pie, the answer here could be either A, B, or D.

An incidental note: True love of chocolate is often directly related to a seeming lack of affection toward it (in public). Studies show that someone who declines even a bite of your chocolate mousse will, in nine cases out of ten, do so while thinking of that box of Devil Dogs and carton of double fudge ice cream awaiting her at home. 72% of women I personally questioned on the subject of chocolate say if they had it to do all over again they would still eat the brownie mix before it was cooked, and 20% tell me to mind my own business. The other 8% have given it up entirely and eat honey instead. Right out of the jar. With a big spoon.

Water Conservation

She insists that to save water you must flush the toilet only once a day. Do you:

A. agree and keep the lid down?

B. stop bathing—supposedly to conserve even more water, but actually in retaliation?

C. rent a Porta-John for your backyard, back porch, or hall closet, and pretend you live at a music festival?

The answer is C. You'll not only save water, you'll meet the nicest strange women in line.

"Hello?"

In the beginning, the telephone was a vital link between you and your lover in those agonizing hours you were forced to spend apart. But now that you're living in the same place, it has become less of a major convenience and more of a minor annoyance. What is the worst time for the phone to ring?

A. During dinner.

B. When one of you is outside and the other is in the bathroom.

C. While the two of you are disagreeing loudly.

D. When the movie will be over in five minutes.

E. During sex.

The answer is C, because in the other situations you would probably both agree to let it keep ringing—or you'd let your phone machine take it. When you're fighting, though, one of you (the one who is losing) will answer it to cut off the discussion and leave the other fuming. Oooh . . . .

In Sickness And In Health

Your lover is in bed with a mild case of the flu. What is the extent of your nursing obligation toward her?

A. Putting the kettle on for tea and handing her the remote control.

B. Taking her temperature, plumping her pillows, and feeding her cups of chicken soup.

C. Waiting on her hand and foot until you collapse.

D. Crawling in beside her and performing a healing technique on her body which is known as "breaking the fever."

E. Hiring a nurse.

C is what your mother would do, E is what your father would do, and A is not quite sympathetic enough. Give yourself a point for B if you're the nurturing type and D if you find the sickroom especially arousing.

Annoying Habits

Which is the most annoying habit for your lover to have?

A. Nail-biting.

B. Snoring.

C. Picking at her zits.

D. Leaving the lid off the marmalade jar.

E. Sleeping with your best friend.

The answer is B, because when she is doing any of the others you are free to leave the room. When she snores, all you can do is roll her over or smother her with her own pillow. Hopefully, it will never come to that. If you are truly in love, you will adjust to it, in the way you can adjust to a train that roars through your living room every morning around three a.m.

Happy, Happy Birthday, Baby

You expect a leather jacket with a fake fur collar for your birthday, and your lover gives you a blender instead. Do you:

A. smile sweetly and exchange it?

B. cry?

C. break up with her immediately?

D. make piña coladas?

The answer is D. Be gracious, and remember it could have been much worse: she could have given you the jacket, and you could've worn it to the bar, and a woman with an eye for leather could've come on to you and made your lover jealous and you could've had a terrible fight and you could've gone home with that woman just for spite and she could've turned out to be just another repressed Catholic and you could've gone home the next morning feeling unnerved and frustrated only to find your lover had packed up and moved in the night. Believe me, you should thank your lucky stars for that blender.

The Holidays — Your Folks Or Mine

On holidays there is always the problem of the "in-laws." Let's say your folks live two hours east of your city or town and her folks live two and a half hours west. How will you be spending Thanksgiving?

A. On the road, running from one set of folks to the other.

B. Visiting her folks, because her mother makes terrific cranberry muffins.

C. Visiting your folks, because your mother will cry if you don't.

D. Under the covers, eating Swanson TV turkey dinners.

E. Each going to your own set of folks and sneaking away from the table before dessert to talk on the phone and wish you were together.

In this situation D is highly advisable, even if you're both vegetarians.

When Her Parents Come To Town, or "Oh, Hi, Mr. And Mrs. Merten, Uh — Bob And Nancy, Uh — Mom And Dad, Uh — Hi"

When your lover's parents come to town (assuming they live somewhere else), what can you do to make their stay as pleasant as possible?

A. Bake lots of high-fiber oatmeal bran cookies.

B. Make love to their daughter as quietly as possible.

C. Wear a dress when you all go out to dinner.

D. Go and stay with friends.

E. Pretend not to notice that her father is attracted to you.

F. Pretend not to notice that her mother is attracted to you.

Probably the best thing to do is B. If this is not possible, the situation could quickly degenerate to a point where they will decide to move to a hotel or, on the other hand, they will both be attracted to you simultaneously. Pretend not to notice.

Listen To The Heartbeat

She drives a two-year-old Subaru. You drive a ten-year-old Chevy. Whose car do you take on vacation?

A. Hers.

B. Yours.

C. Hers, but you drive.

D. Yours, but you both push.

E. Neither—you take the train.

The answer is D. The exercise will be good for you, and a little shared adversity can make your time together even more special. Just be sure to carry plenty of water, warm blankets, and snakebite medicine for those extra special breakdowns in the desert.

"And After The Skunk Sprayed The Tent And I Fell In The Fire, It Began To Rain"

Her idea of camping out is a camouflaged lean-to along the Appalachian Trail. Yours is an air mattress on the deck of a time-sharing condo in Key West. What's the best compromise?

A. Spending a week in the Shenandoah Valley in a log cabin with no indoor plumbing, visiting some dear old separatist friends who still do leather work, drive a VW bus, and think "rap" is what you do in your CR group.

B. Renting an RV complete with shower and microwave and parking it in a campground full of trees and bugs and nature stuff.

C. Riding ten-speeds through the Everglades, where you will have your toe bitten off by an alligator.

D. Staying home and sulking together.

The answer is C. This way she'll get the exercise and fresh air and you'll get the sympathy and the perfect excuse to forego any future adventures along those lines. Next year it's a bed-and-breakfast in P-Town.

Babies — Large Cats Without Fur And Tails

When I was five years old, my mother told me that when you fell in love and decided to have a baby, that's when you asked God and God sent you a baby — which is essentially how lesbians have their babies, if you think of God as a sperm bank. Gee, so how do you suppose my mother knew . . . anyway, here comes this baby. How does it differ from your favorite cat Sadie?

A. Sadie learned to use the litter box when she was five weeks old.

B. Sadie only cries when she's hungry.

C. Sadie doesn't wear tiny socks that go for three bucks a pair.

D. Sadie won't develop an unpleasant heat rash.

E. Sadie will never grow up and send off for college catalogs.

Of course, a baby differs in all these respects from Sadie, so give yourself a point for any of these answers. And if you said (to yourself or out loud), "Yeah, but Sadie will never say 'Ma-ma' or win the Nobel Peace Prize, either," or words to that effect, you get an extra two points. We cat-lovers must learn to acknowledge that even a cat can't do everything.

Little Ones

What do you say to a child to explain the lesbian family?

A. "You have two mommies, dear."

B. "Love is what makes a family."

C. "If Donald teases you on the playground again, just ask him why his father keeps passing out on their front lawn. That'll shut him up."

D. "It's not on TV because TV sucks, that's why."

E. "Sure, honey—Betty Bear could fall in love with Susie Bear."

B. Ah, gee. (You can also use this to explain the lesbian family to your Irish setter.)

The Big Six Months

You've been together for six whole months, and now you begin to notice:

A. how often she's told that story about seeing Dolly Parton in a women's bar in Nashville.

B. that she always seems to let you leave most of the tip for the waitress.

C. none of her ex-lovers are on speaking terms with her.

D. in lovemaking, you know what's coming next.

E. every day you're more gloriously in love than ever.

The answer is E. Not that answers A–D aren't just as sure to be true, but let's be positive. Besides, you've got to make it last, at least through the next three questions.

The Third Year

You've been together for three whole years, and you've reached a relationship plateau. Would you say that:

A. you're so bored you could scream?

B. you wish you could leave, but you can't afford to move right now?

C. it wouldn't be so bad if only she didn't always wear those awful saggy sweatpants around the house?

D. you guess you have to expect a sort of letdown after all this time?

E. every day you're more gloriously in love than ever?

E. (Now remember, we're being positive.)

The Seventh Year

You've been together for seven years (some might say seven *long* years). Your relationship has become a fine blend of comfort and restlessness. It's a good time to renegotiate matters. What's first on the agenda?

A. You'd like to trade ironing for doing the household bills.

B. She'd like to take more weekend trips with you.

C. You'd like to talk about the possibility of an open relationship.

D. She needs to tell you about a woman she's met in her low-impact aerobics class.

E. You just have to say that every day you're more gloriously in love than ever.

F. She wants to have a baby.

E. (I said *positive*. Besides, if she's talking about a baby, you'd better be good and E.)

Beyond Ten (Better Known As "All Eternity")

You've been together for at least ten years. What do you hear the most from other women?

A. "You mean you two still make love?"

B. "You're a real role model for the rest of us."

C. "So if nothing's wrong, why are you both drinking so much?"

D. "The same face on the pillow every morning? I'd go stark raving mad!"

E. "You mean every day you're more gloriously in love than ever?"

The answer is—E. Again. And those of you who refuse to look on the bright side of all four questions either have your sun and several planets in Gemini or you just don't believe in love. Loosen up, girls, it's supposed to be fun.

Happy, Happy Anniversary, Baby

When most women celebrate their anniversary, what day are they so fondly recalling?

A. The day they met.

B. The day they first made love.

C. The day they bought the house.

D. The day they told their parents.

E. The day they got their periods simultaneously.

The most common answer is B, or possibly A, particularly if A and B occurred on the same day. (See? I wasn't even trying to trick you on this one. I was only trying to trick me, because my love and I celebrate A. Just A—after that it's all been a wonderful blur.)

Two Bodies, One Brain

When two women live together intimately for any length of time, they begin to adopt similar mannerisms and patterns of living. How can you tell when this sort of behavior has gotten out of hand?

A. You finish each other's sentences.

B. You are mistaken for each other on the phone.

C. You are mistaken for each other on the street.

D. You wake up one morning and find that your bones have fused together in the night, leaving you permanently joined at the hip.

The answer is C. A and B are only to be expected after a while, and D only occurs in those rare instances where two women become so interdependent that one can't do anything without the other, in which case they will be reading this book together and won't even realize they're joined at the hip. (And then it'll be too late—booga-booga.)

One Gets Rich, The Other Doesn't

What happens when only one of you becomes very successful in her career?

A. You buy the good champagne.

B. You get to travel more often to exotic, erotic places.

C. The successful one leaves.

D. The not-so-successful one leaves.

E. Together you set up a charitable foundation to place homeless canines with loving women and call it "Dogs For Dykes."

E. Happens all the time. I'm sure there's a chapter right in your own neighborhood. If not, you'll get rich and start one.

Open Or Closed
or
"Why Is A Window Like A Love Affair?"

Under what circumstances should you agree to an open relationship?

A. On the first date.

B. The day before you move in with her.

C. The night before she leaves to spend three months in Amsterdam.

D. When she tells you she was faking that last orgasm.

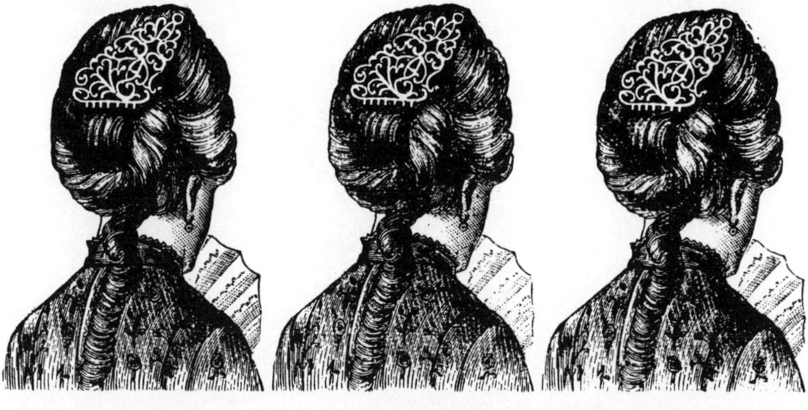

A. This is something you have to get straight (pardon the expression) from the beginning. Later on it will rarely be an idea you can both embrace at the same moment, and when it's not, honey—look out!

The Processing Process

Where is the best place to draw the line on "processing?" Just short of a major discussion of:

A. her sister who's been sleeping on the couch for a month.

B. your feelings about the way she says "Good night" on the phone when you call from out of town.

C. who isn't cleaning the kitty litter.

D. her feelings about your upcoming trip to China with your boss who's also your ex-lover.

E. a control issue, such as that way you always have of picking the movie or the restaurant or the time to make love.

B. Tone of voice discussions are borderline paranoia and lead nowhere. Kitty litter, when it is dirty, can become very important.

"Oh, Yeah?"

What is the most effective thing to say during an argument if you wish to drive your lover bug-eyed crazy?

A. "Sez you."

B. "Big deal."

C. "I never said that."

D. "I can't argue with anyone who has an intimacy problem as serious as yours."

E. "I'm rubber, you're glue."

D runs a close second, but C is best—only you must use it in response to her repeating something you actually *did* say not more than ten minutes before. Unless she's taping the entire conversation, how's she going to prove it? Heh-heh . . . .

"Hmmm — And How Does That Make You Feel?"

Most couples you and I know who go for couples counseling break up within a few weeks of their first session. This has become so common that to announce you and your lover are in counseling together is practically the verbal equivalent of mailing out a formal separation notice. What is the reason for this?

A. Couples wait until they're on the verge of breaking up to go to a counselor.

B. The counselor can see right off the bat that they can't agree on anything, their goals and priorities are diametrically opposed, they aren't even compatible in bed, and the relationship is senseless, impossible, and hopeless—and she tells them so.

C. The counselor talks a lot about compromise and communication and cooperation while the two women sit there, each thinking "but I *did*" and "but I *tried*" and "but she *won't*." Then they thank the counselor and write her a check and go home and break up.

D. It's all the counselor's fault—they were doing fine until she came along and stuck her nose into their personal business.

E. More than half of these couples who say they're going for counseling are really just going to the movies and lying about it.

The answer is D. Not really, but go ahead and blame her if it makes you feel better. She won't mind, she's learned detachment.

"I Didn't Plan To Fall In Love — It Just Happened"

The love of your life comes to you and announces she is in love with a woman you both know. She tells you, "We didn't plan to fall in love — it just happened." What do you reply?

A. "I know just what you mean—I can't tell you how often that's happened to me."

B. "Good luck then, darling."

C. "Oh, I'll just bet it did."

D. "Why (her name), I didn't know you had taken to reading Harlequin romances."

E. "That's the absolute sorriest excuse for switching partners I ever heard in my life."

F. "Get out of here, Vida, before I kill you."

The answer is G, all of the above (I just forgot to list it). During the course of the breakup, you will either start with A and work your way through to F, or go from F backwards. It all depends on whether you hold your anger in for a while or let it fly. Either way, you really shouldn't let her get away with it. "It just happened." Come on . . . .

When Your New Love Leaves You For Your Old, And Variations Thereof

All right, granted, the lesbian community, even in a good-sized city, can become pretty incestuous after a few years, and you do have to be prepared for any one of a number of possibly uncomfortable and/or heart-breaking developments. Of the following, which scenario would you find the most difficult to handle emotionally?

A. If your lover of six months left you for your old lover, the one you had left to be with the new one.

B. If your lover left you to be with your nurse-practitioner but came back to you after one night.

C. If you left your lover to be with *her* old lover and then began sleeping with them both, but within weeks the two of them got back together and dropped *you*.

D. If you finally got back together with an old lover, and soon she left you for your mother and they built a house and asked you to come for Christmas.

It would probably be a toss-up between C and D. A point for C (the sort of situation that might cause an otherwise happy-go-lucky dyke to turn to televangelism) and condolences and two points for D (the stuff of which Greek tragedy is made).

Photographic Evidence

Within days of the breakup, you're trying to pack and sort and get on with your life. You come upon a box of photographs: some she took of you in the bathtub, some you took of her at Disneyworld, and some of the two of you together at a cookout. How should you divide them up?

A. With a pair of garden shears.

B. You take the ones you took, leave her the ones she took, and pick out several of the two of you together to keep for old times' sake.

C. You take the ones she took and leave her the rest.

D. You leave her all of them.

Always C. Always, always, always. If after you've both cooled out (assuming you do) she wants to share some of the others with you, fine—but get those bathtub shots, or you'll be wondering who'll see them and where they could turn up (including in "The National Enquirer") for the rest of your natural life.

In Recovery

You'll know you've recovered from the breakup when:

A. you can drive to work and not think every red Honda you glimpse out of the corner of your eye is hers.

B. you don't cry yourself to sleep anymore.

C. you dump the woman you left her for.

D. your therapist says so.

E. you've stopped plotting revenge.

D. Because you may not recognize the signs. Also, you may recover and still continue plotting revenge.

Sleeping With Your Ex

Now it's been a while since you ended a relationship. You and your ex have let go of your anger and hurt feelings and are having lunch together. It brings back a lot of warm, tender feelings for you both. Do you:

A. smile and suggest another nice lunch in the near future?

B. take her hand and lead her back to your new apartment where you make mad, passionate love?

C. order a second helping of the amaretto cheesecake?

D. ask out the waitress right in front of her?

The answer is A (with C being unnecessarily fattening and D being just plain tacky). Sleeping with an ex can be a tricky thing. To understand why, we must look first at the origin of the word "ex," which comes from the Latin "*ex*," meaning, "I hope we can still be friends." Hope, yes; but there is no guarantee. And renewing a sexual relationship with an ex has been known to send many a woman screaming down the street. Ideally, after a few very pleasant lunches you could make love again, just once (or maybe twice), as a healing sort of gesture and a way of establishing a new bond of affection between you. Ideally. But don't count on a reconciliation. More likely, you'll find it rather disturbing that she's learned to be multi-orgasmic without you.

Here We Go Again
or
Patterns Are Only Nice For Quilts

Every relationship you've ever been in starts like a house afire, quickly evolves into the greatest love of all, and abruptly ends within the first year. Do you discern a pattern here?

A. I know, I know—I can't help myself.

B. What do you mean "pattern?" You mean like those McCall's things? Ooh, I hated those. I never had enough cloth to cut out all the pieces. Home Ec, ninth grade. Yuck. What was the question?

C. No. No, not really.

D. I just have a knack for picking the wrong people.

E. I'm atoning for my sins in a past life.

C. If this has been happening to you repeatedly for some years, you won't even notice anymore.

PART IV

Living In Your World, The World At Large, And Worlds Beyond

Celibacy

You've remained celibate for six months. Do you ask your friends to:

A. stop giving you vibrators?

B. stop giving you phone numbers?

C. talk you out of it?

D. all of the above?

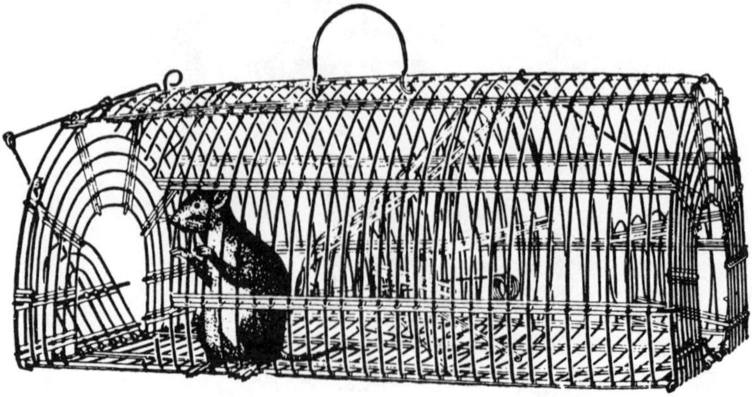

The answer is C. You asked them to B after two months and A after four months. After six months, celibacy almost always loses its charm. Regrouping your sexual energy is one thing—throwing in the towel is quite another.

Your Single Friend

You have a friend who is usually single because her relationships never last more than a few months — or in some cases, a few days. She says it's because she hates sleeping with another body in the bed — it's too hot. Why do *you* think it is?

A. Her lovers have told her that her body is too hot to sleep with in a bed.

B. She's just not the marrying kind.

C. Once she's slept with someone, she totally loses her identity for as long as the affair continues (which isn't long, my pretty, which isn't long).

D. Some women who are fantastic friends make terrible lovers.

E. She's secretly in love with you.

D. There's nothing like a little intimacy to make a good woman go bad.

Being Friends With The Lovers Of Your Friends

Why is it so tricky to be friends with your friend's lover?

A. All of the below.

B. It's no use getting close to her, because when they break up you'll never see her again.

C. If you don't particularly care for her, and you take your friend's side during one of their spats, when they get back together all your friend will remember is that *you* said something unkind about her own true love.

D. If you get too close to her, you may both find there's a strong mutual attraction, and this will put a terrible strain on everybody.

E. After they break up your friend's now ex-lover may ask you out, and your friend will tell you to do whatever you want, but when you do go out with her ex she'll stop speaking to you and that will make you feel awful so you'll tell the ex you can't date her again and *she'll* get mad and stop speaking to you, too, and there you'll be.

The answer is often A. I don't say it's always A, but I do say it's tricky. It will also depend a lot on how quickly your friends tend to run through lovers.

Donna Juanita Syndrome

Why do some girls seem to have such a strong need for sexual conquests?

A. They were born that way.

B. They couldn't get a date in high school.

C. They crave new and exciting experiences that don't involve jumping out of airplanes.

D. They're writing a book.

E. Sex burns calories.

My theory is D—and they may tell you they're going to change all the names and dates and no one will ever recognize you, but they lie. This is why you should avoid them at all costs when they unzip your tent flap and bat their eyes and say, "Hi—mind if I sleep here tonight?"

Overnight Guests

A dear old ex-lover and her new girlfriend are traveling cross-country in their camper van and stop to spend the night at your place. Sounds like fun, doesn't it? But what's the worst that could happen?

A. Their dog will chew up one of your new Reeboks.

B. Their van will leak three quarts of oil in your driveway.

C. Your ex will do the dishes and break your favorite cup.

D. The new girlfriend will come on to you.

E. The nuclear plant fifty miles upwind of you will have a major meltdown.

E. The best thing you can say for nuclear accidents is they put all our little worries in perspective.

"And Then I Realize It's Dr. Ruth, And She's Ripping Off My —"

When you have an erotic dream about someone other than your present lover, do you:

A. tell your lover immediately, in graphic detail?

B. refrain from telling your lover about it and feel a little guilty?

C. keep it to yourself and use it to brighten many a boring afternoon at work?

D. find the woman in your erotic dream and insist on telling *her* about it, even if the woman happens to be Cher?

E. wonder why in dreams like that no one's ever having her period?

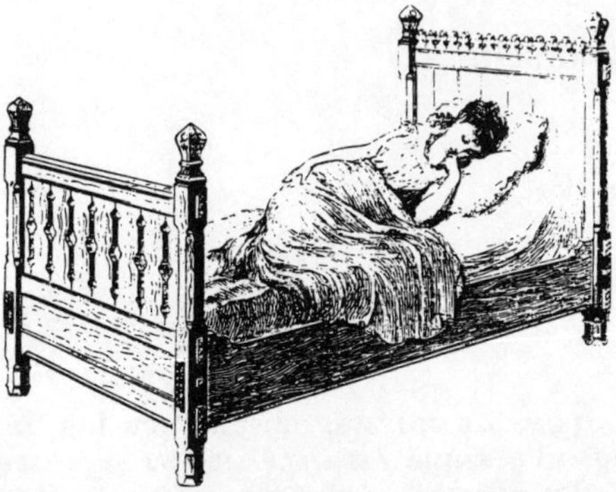

C. Isn't that what dreams are for?

Bright Lights, Big City

You are moving from a quaint village with a population of 650 (and a grand total of 65 gay people, only three of whom are out, even to themselves) to a teeming metropolis of 650,000 (whose population contains 65,000 gay people, with maybe 20,000 (33% or so) out to themselves and various other segments of society). What's the biggest adjustment you'll have to make when settling in?

A. Paying an exorbitant rent.

B. Having nowhere to park your car.

C. Locking your doors, your windows, and your bicycle, and chaining your geranium to the shelf on the back porch.

D. Never knowing who your neighbors are until after they've been arrested.

E. Being yourself.

The answer is E. I think. Take a half-credit for A-D, because city living does take some getting used to. Being yourself, and as a gay woman even discovering who that is, is not always easy either, but the rewards are well worth the effort. I'm not sure the rewards are well worth the rent, though.

Out Of The Ghetto And Into The 'Burbs

How does living in the suburbs differ from living in a primarily gay neighborhood of a major city?

A. Your dog is more constipated in the city.

B. You are more constipated in the suburbs.

C. In the city you get more dates.

D. In the suburbs you get fewer pigeons on the bird feeder.

E. All of the above.

The only gross generalization we can be sure of here is D. If you're a big birdlover, this could be a primary factor in your decision of where to live. Other than that, it all depends on you. And your dog. And your fiber intake.

Collectively Speaking

How are decisions made in a women's collective?

A. After a thorough discussion of the issue, a course of action is proposed and accepted by a majority vote.

B. The issue is turned over to a steering committee for further discussion, but the committee can never find a good time they can all meet except Sunday afternoon—and no one wants to meet then.

C. Everyone expresses her opinion on the issue, but no one listens to Jade's opinion anymore because she's sleeping with someone outside the collective.

D. Elena chairs the meeting, and whoever wants to stay in the group does whatever Elena says.

E. They close the door for privacy and then flip a coin.

B is the answer that can best be applied to most collectives. This is why they're always in the process of getting back to you. If you are very lucky, a decision will be made in your lifetime.

Where Have All The Separatists Gone?

I wonder if you've noticed this: a significant number of those women you knew in the seventies who were hard-line separatists, drastic dykes, and devotees of "The Clit Papers" and other manifestos against the patriarchy have turned in their overalls and married men and had babies. What do you suppose causes this strange phenomenon?

A. Some people will do anything for attention.

B. It's so hard to be a separatist that when you get exhausted you throw up your hands and say "Ah, fuck it, I give up!"

C. Their hearts were in the right place, but they weren't really lesbians to begin with.

D. Men can support them in a style to which they have *not* become accustomed.

E. They've been kidnapped, drugged, and brainwashed by the FBI.

B, probably (although if it's E we'll never know, will we?). Separatism is like any form of fundamentalist ideology. It works really well in your own house, but outside it clearly has its limitations. But the irony here is that those same girls who stopped speaking to you because you refused to stop speaking to your brother are now not speaking to you because you can't relate to economy-sized boxes of Pampers. Well, you can never please some people.

I've Got All Your Records, or "Guess Who I Slept With In 1982 When She Was Warming Up For Cris Williamson?"

It's a curious thing, but the music business does seem to have a way of attracting groupies, and in a slightly more subtle fashion, this holds true in the lesbian community just as well as it does backstage after an Aerosmith concert. Why is this so?

A. Women musicians are inherently more sensuous than you are.

B. Women musicians lead you to believe they are inherently more sensuous than you are.

C. Most women musicians are either highly evolved spiritual beings or the sleaziest dregs of womankind, and you can't always tell who's who until the next morning. That's what makes it so exciting.

D. Because we often make love while listening to music, the majority of songs are love songs, and music is all rhythm and motion and climax, we've come to equate music with sex.

E. Music *is* sex.

The answer is D. Now I have nothing personal against love songs—some of my best friends write them. But let's try to remember that those who cannot tell the singer from the song often end up on the sidewalk with the puzzled looks on their afterglowing faces when the loaded van with the bad shocks pulls away from the curb. (Additional warning: And don't quit your day job and pack your bags and move out to California to be near her. Her live-in girlfriend won't like that one bit.)

S And M

You don't hear very much about S and M now. Why do you suppose that is?

A. The S and M dykes quit writing letters to the gay newspapers.

B. It's so hard to find a decent set of restraints these days.

C. It made too many women giggle.

D. It's old hat—the latest is S and L.

E. Women got tired of trying to sleep in spiked dog collars.

D. The latest is S and L. Sweetness and Lust. During a session of S and L you're *supposed* to giggle.

Birth Control

Imagine what it would be like if every time you and your honey made love you had to worry about whether or not you were being careful enough not to make a baby. Wow — what a weird concept. But just suppose: if lesbians had to use birth control, what form would the contraceptive take?

A. Chocolate foam.

B. A pill whose only possible side-effect is an occasional involuntary smile.

C. Mind control.

D. An organically grown diaphragm that, upon insertion, expands directly over the G-spot.

C, which is already the form of birth control we use, or we'd all be having babies by parthenogenesis.

Oh, Give Me An Ommmmm

When they meditate or chant, lesbians have been known to:

A. Fall asleep.

B. Hear their stomachs growling.

C. Have orgasms.

D. Attain a state of bliss.

E. Be unable to concentrate because they're wondering why their partners are an hour late arriving at the ashram.

C. This happens. Not to me personally, but then I can't meditate for more than thirty seconds without my nose itching.

Odd Hygiene Facts #2

So — we come in all shapes and sizes, races and creeds, from every background and on our way toward every walk of life. However ... in all your experience, have you ever encountered a lesbian who douched?

A. Yes, I have.

B. No, I haven't.

C. Just once, but she was an advertising executive who practically invented Summer's Eve.

D. She swore she didn't, but nobody's vagina tastes like vinegar all by itself.

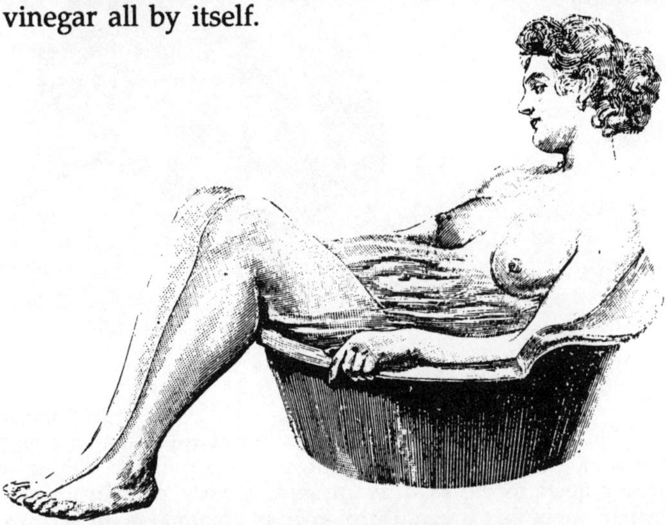

The answer is D. Yes, she did swear, and no, it doesn't.

"Give Up?"

Do you find that now more than ever your friends and lovers are restricting their intake of practically everything? Sure you do. Are they lengthening their lifespans? Probably. Are they cleansing their bodies and purifying their souls? Could be. Are they improving their dispositions? Not on your life. Giving up which of these substances will turn a kind and loving woman into a surly wretch overnight?

A. Coffee.

B. Sugar.

C. Alcohol.

D. Cigarettes.

E. Meat.

F. Sex.

G. Cocaine.

B, sugar. Within minutes of simply making that decision to turn down the next macaroon offered, hundreds of women we all know and love have been known to snap, scream, take furtive bites out of small animals, froth at the mouth, and fall down dead. Such a sudden and violent reaction could only be the result of a dangerous addiction with a strong psychological component.

Telling The World

A famous lesbian tells you to come out to everyone in the world including your dry cleaner. What do you do?

A. Come out to your family.

B. Come out to your neighbors and co-workers.

C. Come out to everyone in the world including your dry cleaner.

D. Tell the famous lesbian where she can stick it.

The answer is, of course, D. It's always up to *you* and your personal comfort level as to how "out" you want to be. Not being a famous lesbian myself I am only guessing, but it must be awfully easy to tell other women how to live their lives and put their jobs and/or security on the line after you already got yours. (And it's funny how accepting straight people can be once they've seen you on "Good Morning, America.") When you live in Minneapolis and teach seventh grade it's a little bit different, so you act accordingly. (Now if I ever do become a famous lesbian, I hope you'll remind me I said this—and I'll do the same for you sometime.)

Why Famous Dykes Don't Tell

We'll have to speculate here. But while in the previous question we can understand why the teacher in Minneapolis hesitates before shouting her lifestyle from the rooftops, it seems less clear why all but a couple of the famous dykes (and there are tons of them) never mention it when they're on "Good Morning, America," since it would be so helpful in broadening and enlightening a homophobic society's narrow picture of who lesbians are. So why don't they?

A. Because they aren't dying of AIDS.

B. Because they don't want to be spokeswomen for lesbians as a group.

C. Because they haven't finished their autobiographies.

D. Because they're very private individuals.

E. Because they're scared shitless of ruining their careers.

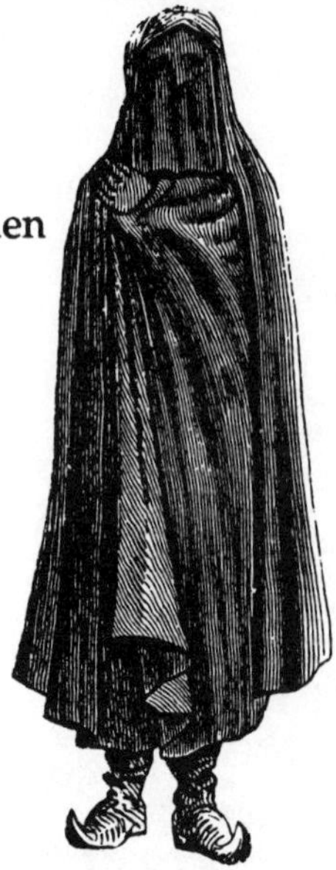

They will tell you the answer is B or D. Well, who are we to judge? But if any famous dykes out there are considering telling (for the umpteenth time), may I just suggest that if it's too much for you to handle while you live, why not prepare a nice video or written statement to be released after your death? That couldn't hurt your autobiography, your privacy, or your career, could it? Okay, we won't push . . . .

Lives Past And Future Perfect

Your lover tells you she's realized the two of you were together in a past life, and her feeling is that you were sisters. What is your reply?

A. "And we'll always be together, darling, throughout all eternity."

B. "Well, they say incest is relative."

C. "Okay, I'll buy that—but which of us was Cleopatra?"

D. "But I can't stand either one of my sisters."

E. "Does this mean George Bush could've been our brother?"

Oh, why not—make it A. It's a nice thought. But, you say, what if there are several other women in my life so far (and maybe more to come—I mean, you never know), and I'd like to think the same thing about them, that we'd all be out there floating around and communing or coming back again and being loving and nobody'd get jealous or feel left out—would that be possible? Certainly. The universe has a way of working these things out, so I'm sure you'll all have a swell time and space (whatever time and space may turn out to be).

The Woman Upstairs

Is there really a Goddess in heaven?

A. Maybe, maybe not.

B. Yeah, but she's more of a spirit, a higher power, than she is an actual Being.

C. Yes, and we were made in Her image. Sometimes, when she works out, she looks a whole lot like Martina.

D. Look, I got enough of this crap from the nuns, so drop it, okay?

E. Guess we'll find out when we get there.

C. And other times she looks just like Amelia Earhart. Or Bessie Smith. Or however you perceive her. She's flexible.

Back To The Amazons

How long will generations of lesbians remain on this planet?

A. Till we get good and fed up.

B. Till it gets to be a civilized place.

C. Till the boys blow it to Kingdom Come.

D. Till the rivers all run dry.

E. Till a week from Saturday.

Probably B or C, whichever comes first. Because we're already good and fed up, aren't we? I know I am. But at least we're here together, girls. That's what makes it all worthwhile.

Scoring

Well, here we are, nearing the end of our journey. Are you tired? Are you exhilarated? And more importantly, what is that leaking out of your backpack?

I'm sure that by now all my readers have realized a number of things—first, that there are more aspects and elements to the lesbian lifestyle than you can shake a stick at, and in these 101 questions we've only scratched the surface; second, that if you had been leading this expedition you might have taken us another way round, on the happy trails only you know best; and finally, that it is just possible I was making up these answers as I went along. Any one of these conclusions is probably true—and yet, since the topics I chose to point out along the way were those closest to my heart and funnybone, it seems fair that I should decide on the answers. (Now if only life were like that—and then again, perhaps it is.) What I'm trying to say is I hope you didn't take this scoring business too seriously, because my personal opinions (though keenly insightful, if I do say so myself) cannot be construed as an exact science, and my math's not too good, either. However, if you insist on being competitive, I won't stop you. (I only hope you'll win an interesting side bet with your dearest—something that would involve a silk sheet and a can of whipped cream.)

Give yourself one point for each correct response (now that sounds simple enough), with half-credits or extra points as they pertain to individual questions. Add up your good points, work on your not-so-good ones, and rate yourself according to the following chart.

75–100 or more	SuperDyke (probably cheated)
50–75	My Kind of Woman (trying too hard)
25–50	An Average Jo (oh, like in "Little Women?")
0–25	TV Generation With Short Attention Span (wishes you'd put down the book and pick *her* up)
Less than 0	Careless (meant to add instead of subtract)

Whatever your score, I hope it's been fun for you. I know I've had a swell time. Now if only life were like this—and then again, perhaps it is . . . .